THE
Archive Photographs
SERIES

CHESTER

Once an everyday scene, The Cross is now a pedestrian way with access only available for delivery transport. The sign attached to the corner of St Peter's church shows the old route to the A 5116 to Birkenhead.

THE
Archive Photographs
SERIES

CHESTER

Compiled by
Michael Day and Pat O'Brien

TEMPUS

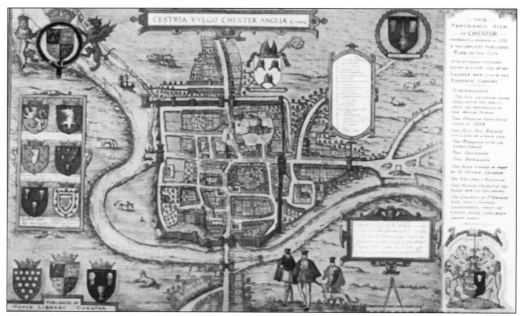

This is the earliest known plan of the city, dated 1572 and this copy was published by Hukes Library. The six heraldic coats of arms were those of the Norman earls of the city. (See page 48)

First published 1996
Reprinted 2004

Tempus Publishing Limited
The Mill, Brimscombe Port,
Stroud, Gloucestershire, GL5 2QG
www.tempus-publishing.com

British Library Cataloguing in Publication Data.
A catalogue record for this book is available from the British Library.

ISBN 0 7524 0681 7

Typesetting and origination by Tempus Publishing Limited.
Printed in Great Britain.

Contents

CORONATION

OF HER  MAJESTY

QUEEN VICTORIA.

PROGRAMME

OF

THE CHARITY SCHOOLS

OF THE CITY OF CHESTER.

THE Citizens, with their accustomed attention to the rising generation, having resolved, that the gratification and comfort of the Children shall form one of the principal parts of the festivities of this auspicious day, the Sub-committee appointed to carry out this design, have adopted the following arrangements:—The Children, each bringing a Knife and Fork, will assemble in their various Schools at an early hour, and proceed at Eight o'clock to the places assigned to each in the LINEN HALL, the Knives and Forks will then be laid where each Child will sit to Dine, from thence they will proceed to the Castle Yard, assembling there at Nine o'clock. Before the Procession starts from the Castle Yard, the Choir from the Cathedral will sing the National Anthem, the various Schools joining in chorus.

| God save our gracious Queen, Long live our noble Queen, God save the Queen! Send her victorious, Happy and glorious, Long to reign over us, God save the Queen! | O Lord our God arise, Scatter her enemies, And make them fall: Confound their politics, Frustrate their knavish-tricks, On her our hopes we fix, God save us all! | Thy choicest gifts in store Still on Victoria pour, Long may she reign: May she defend our laws, And ever give us cause To sing with heart and voice, God save the Queen! | Shield her thou God and Great, And to our Church and State New blessings design: Guard Britain's Throne, and long May the exulting throng, For them renew the song, God save the Queen! |

The Schools will walk immediately after the First Band, in the following order:—

	BOYS.	GIRLS.	TOTAL.
Garrison School	37	25	62

SUNDAY SCHOOLS.

	BOYS.	GIRLS.	TOTAL.		BOYS.	GIRLS.	TOTAL.
1 Presbyterian Chapel	26	—	26	8 Independents			440
2 Cambrian and Northgate Street	30	40	70	Viz.—Queen Street	120	140	
3 Primitive Methodist	30	55	85	Handbridge	55	45	
4 Octagon Chapel (Lady Huntington's)	60	70	130	Boughton	42	88	
5 Commonhall Street	61	83	144	Church of England			680
6 New Connexion Methodists			358	Viz.—			
Viz.—Goss Street	76	100		9 Saint Michael's and St. Martin's	18	28	
Brown Street	87	95		10 Saint Bridget's	29	25	
7 Wesleyan Methodists			378	11 Saint Oswald's	70	50	
Viz.—St. John Street	72	86		12 Saint Mary's	90	91	
Brook Street	110	110		13 Trinity			
				14 St. Paul's	41	74	

DAY SCHOOLS.

	BOYS.	GIRLS.	TOTAL.		BOYS.	GIRLS.	TOTAL.
15 Saint Paul's	130	125	255	17 Consolidated Girls' School	—	100	100
16 Diocesan	160	—	160	18 Marquis Westminster	230	170	400
19 Roman Catholics	50	60	110				

The following Schools will walk after the Ancient Companies:—

	BOYS.	GIRLS.	TOTAL.		BOYS.	GIRLS.	TOTAL.
20 Blue Girls' School	—	23	23	21 Blue and Green Boys	88	—	88
22 King's School	24	—	24				

Schools to Remain at Home.

	BOYS.	GIRLS.	TOTAL.		BOYS.	GIRLS.	TOTAL.
Kale Yard, Infants	54	72	126	Handbridge, Infants	48	52	100
Boughton, Infants	50	43	93	House of Industry	47	44	91

The total number of Children receiving gratuitous education in the City of Chester, at the present time, is 3912; viz., in Sunday Schools, 2281; in Day Schools, 1631.

EIGHT HUNDRED and SEVENTY-TWO of the above number, being nearly all under Six years of age, will not walk in the Procession, but receive a large Bun and a Medal at School.

THREE THOUSAND and FORTY of the above number will walk, furnished with Medals, when the Procession reaches the Watergate, the Schools will turn off into the Linen Hall, where they will sit down to dinner. 120 pieces of beef of 15 pounds each, 218 plum puddings of 7 pounds each, with bread, &c., will be served up for the occasion cold. The Children will sing the following, accompanied by a bugle:—

| BEFORE DINNER.—TUNE—Old Hundred. Be present at our table Lord, Be here and everywhere adored, These creatures bless, and grant that we May feast in Paradise with Thee. | AFTER DINNER. TUNE—Anvers. We thank Thee Lord for this our food, But most of all for Jesus blood, Let manna to our souls be giv'n, The Bread of Life sent down from Heav'n. |

The following Anthem, composed for the occasion by J. VAUGHAN, will then be sung by the children, the band and teachers joining in chorus, after which they will return to their Schools, and be dispersed:—

JOHN HOPE, Honorary Secretary to Sub-Committee.

Eastman's butchers were situated at No. 52 Northgate Street from about 1903 until 1925, when they moved down the street to No. 34.

Introduction

Modern Chester has its roots in two thousand years of history. Scattered about the city are a myriad of artefacts from different historical periods; one such is the Roman amphitheatre, but Norman architecture can be found within the Cathedral and St John's church, as well as in the fourteenth century Rows. The Tudor House is reputed to be one of the oldest buildings in the city but splendid Tudor, Georgian and Victorian buildings are located throughout Chester.

This book, however, deals with the last 150 years of the city's history and could best be described as 'within recent memory'. It is a document that remembers changes that have been described by grandparents and parents or even witnessed by ourselves. So much has changed in the name of progress. Occasionally such progress unearths relics of the past, such as a Roman mosaic floor but the trend has been for demolition and destruction: even the Anchorite's cell of 1358 is now irretrievably altered.

In this essentially social history of the city and its environs, the residents of Chester and their way of life are recorded and remembered. There were many local photographers in Chester. Not all are represented here but among those whose work is pictured are T. Chidley, Mark Cook and W.S. Garrad. It is interesting to note that Chester was home to over a dozen local postcard publishers as well as to a variety of national ones. The images in this book recall not just the city itself but also the people who were born, lived, worked and died in the area. The text is only a guideline; it is hoped that the pictures included will evoke memories that have long lain hidden in the reader's mind, such memories will enhance the pleasure of reading the book.

The sight of people visiting King Charles I Tower is is still a common one today. The chimney in the background is long gone. It belonged to a small iron foundry called the Providence Foundry, owned by H. Lancely and Son, situated in Newton.

One

Within and Without the Walls

The mayor and his civic party went by boat from the Groves, up river, to Heronbridge, where they disembarked. With assistance, Mayor Hugh Dutton stood on the boundary stone and told of the ancient tradition of bumping a Bluecoat boy on the stone. In some towns a boy was beaten at each stone in order to imprint its location upon his memory, hence the phrase, 'beating the bounds'! The area embraced within the bounds of Chester was 2,000 acres.

This is the second Primitive Methodist church to be built in George Street; the first one is still there, down near Gorse Stacks. This one was built in the late 1800s at a cost of £7,500 and survived until 1955. The gates in the foreground still face what was once Victoria Road.

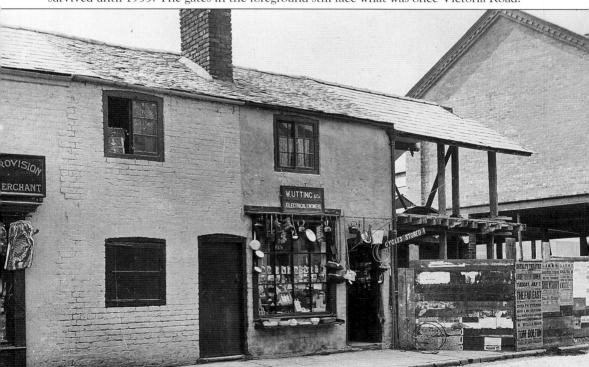

The back of this photograph identifies it as the bottom of George Street. Posters advertise 'Variety Entertainment' with Tom Bolton at the Royalty Theatre on Tuesday 7 July and an L & NW railway excursion to a military tournament at Shrewsbury.

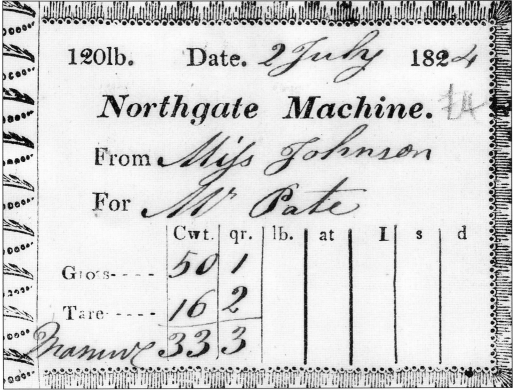

120lb.   Date. *2 July* 182*4*

Northgate Machine. *H*

From *Miss Johnson*

For *Mr Pate*

	Cwt.	qr.	lb.	at	l	s	d
Gross----	50	1					
Tare ----	16	2					
Drawn	33	3					

From 1321 tolls were imposed at all the city gates such as Northgate, below, on anything brought into or taken out of the city. If the payment of a toll was refused, the gate keeper was authorized to take the bridle off the horse. The last time that this happened, the horse ran off and caused chaos, so in 1835 the custom was abolished.

Northgate, Chester.

On the left is the old Liverpool Arms before it was altered. Its previous names were the Dog and Partridge, the Bull and Dog and, in 1789, The Loggerheads Tavern.

John's the tailors came to No. 124 Northgate Street in 1908, while R. Leach, stationers and tobacconists, was established at No. 122 in 1926. Both shops remained until 1929 so this photograph can be dated between 1926 and 1929.

Although the Olde Bell has written on it 'licensed in 1494', licensing was not introduced until 1551. The earliest innkeeper recorded was William Bird, who was made a member of the Innkeeper's Guild on 17 January 1596.

This was the interior of the Blue Bell between 1919 and 1928.

Seen here is Annie Hodgson. She and her sister Edith ran the pub for many years when their father Thomas was the licensee. The Hodgson family had connections with the Blue Bell from 1826 until 1924.

The 'Cabin', seen on the right, was occupied by a hairdresser from 1905 until 1928. W.C. Eaves was its tenant from 1909 until 1919 (see p. 13) and A.E. Backhouse from 1919, as seen here.

C.H. Arden, the butchers shop seen here on the left, had been at No. 132 Northgate Street since about 1909 but is not registered in the 1939 Trade Directory. This would seem to indicate that Northgate Street was resurfaced somewhere between 1929 and 1939. The cottage next to the Blue Bell in 1934 was a shop, occupied in that year by Gerald Kingsman, confectioner and tobacconist.

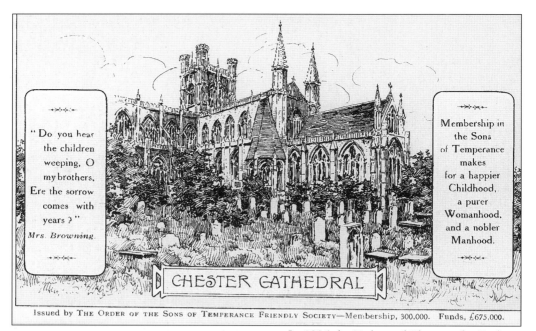

"Do you hear the children weeping, O my brothers, Ere the sorrow comes with years?"

Mrs. Browning.

Membership in the Sons of Temperance makes for a happier Childhood, a purer Womanhood, and a nobler Manhood.

CHESTER CATHEDRAL

Issued by THE ORDER OF THE SONS OF TEMPERANCE FRIENDLY SOCIETY—Membership, 300,000. Funds, £675,000.

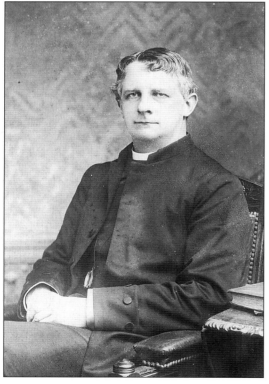

In 1896 the Bishop of Chester, the Right Revd Francis Jayne (left), launched the People's Refreshment Houses Association, financed by £1 shares upon which the maximum return was between five per cent and seven and a half per cent. To prevent infiltration from brewers and drinkers, every shareholder had only one vote. The PRHA opened or bought up and improved public houses in England and Wales; by 1901 it had eighteen where one could buy tea, coffee, temperance drinks and light refreshments, as easily as beer or spirits.

In the Cathedral, on the north side of the nave, a figure carved in the stonework can be seen high up by a window. Tradition states that it is 'Satan in chains', symbolic of the supremacy of the church over evil. Satan is supposed to have been overcome, bound and turned into stone upon seeing so much devotion in the sacred building. The lower picture shows a model of the original.

The scaffolding against the south transept shows that its restoration by Sir Gilbert Scott is still in progress at the time of this photograph. Much of the original exterior has now been altered beyond recognition, and not to everyone's satisfaction.

The Market Hall was opened in 1863. Here monthly fairs of Cheshire cheese were held and the markets regulated the prices. The Hall was also used every Wednesday and Saturday for a general market. A very small part of this facade was retained when the market was demolished in 1967.

This is an advertisement card for the Doric Hotel in Hunter Street, the proprietor of which, from 1909 to 1910, was Mr Thomas Ball. The building is still there, but is now occupied by, among others, Aldersley Hall, florists and the Shropshire Arms, public house.

W.H. Lynn of Belfast, who designed the Town Hall, also designed the Parliament Houses and Government Offices in New South Wales, Australia. Today an addition can be seen on the tower: a clock face has been mounted on three sides to commemorate the 1,900 Anniversary of the City of Chester which took place in 1979. The clock was not installed until 1980.

The Market Place in 1910, when a two-horse omnibus operated – at infrequent intervals – from the Market Square to the Bache. The floor of the lower deck was covered in straw and the upper deck had the old fashioned 'knife board' seats.

The chemists shop in this picture is that of Sangster; in the view above it is Milling's. Further down the street on the right is the Vienna Dining and Tea Room.

On the left can be seen Campbell's light cake shop where cakes and muffins were made by Mr Campbell and later, by his son, on a brick copper standing in one corner of the shop. The family occupied rooms at the rear.

The family of Denson were better known at one time as bakers. In 1869 Robert Denson had a milliners and dressmakers shop in Northgate Street Row. This is an advertisement postcard issued in the early 1900s for a Denson shop in the same area.

This wonderfully ornate front graced a pub, the Masonic Arms in Northgate Street. Its nickname was 'The Muggeries'. In the early part of this century the publican was Mrs Wynne. The site was later occupied by Quaintways.

A view looking up Northgate Street around 1908. At the corner is the Etonian Economic Clothing Co., while at the foot of the steps is a little boy in a push chair at the entrance to Dark Row where a notice board states 'J. Rogers, Registrar of Births, Deaths and Marriages'. The next shop, at No. 147, is Debac and Sheaff, tea and grocers.

The young lady on the left is looking down from the start of Watergate Row North, outside the Victoria Hotel. The policeman at The Cross has just allowed traffic coming from Bridge Street to enter Eastgate Street or Northgate Street in this view from about 1910.

Street traders at one time would resort to the Rows to display and sell their goods. Down in the streets pedestrians had to negotiate a passage on the narrow pavement obstructed by dealers' goods, through streets jammed with horse traffic, and in close proximity, probably, to a variety of obnoxious smells.

Here, at the top of Watergate Street around the turn of the century, we have on street level: Arthur Wall, family butcher, William Peter's (late Nevitts) fish, game and poultry and Arthan, butcher. On the Row: Robert's, the first door up the steps and the Victoria Dining Rooms, established in 1854.

At one time Watergate Street Row South was occupied mainly by candlemakers, thus giving rise to the name Candlemakers Row. The street level premises are reputed at one time to have been used as bonded warehouses in conjunction with the Custom House at the bottom of the street.

Bishop Lloyd was Bishop of Sodor and Man (1599-1605) and of Chester (1605-1615). The date attributed to the house, 1615, is the year in which he died. His grandson was Elihu Yale, born 5 April 1649 in Boston, Massachusetts. Because of donations that Elihu made to the Conneticut College, it changed its name to Yale College in 1718. The photograph below shows his tomb outside Wrexham Parish church.

Where long he liv'd and thriv'd, in London Dead,
Much good some ill he did, so hope all's even
And that his soul through mercy's gone to heaven.

TOMB OF "ELIUGH YALE, ESQ."

Parry & Son, printers, seen here in Watergate Street. In 1869 they occupied premises at No. 98 Eastgate Street. They were were well known throughout the city for their work.

At the bottom end, on the corner of St Nicholas Street, can be seen Holy Trinity church, the only church within the walls with a spire.

In 1780 the Yacht Inn was leased by Bishop Lloyd's house and the landlord was Simon Leet. Residing in the houses in Nicholas Street were, at this time, families of some standing, each retaining a butler, one or more coachmen and domestic staff.

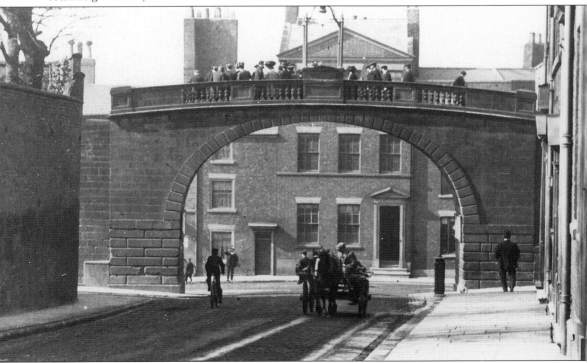

After the Dee was transformed into a navigation channel in the 1730s, the area below the gate took its name fom the recovered land, Sealand. What you see here, beyond the Watergate, is now all gone.

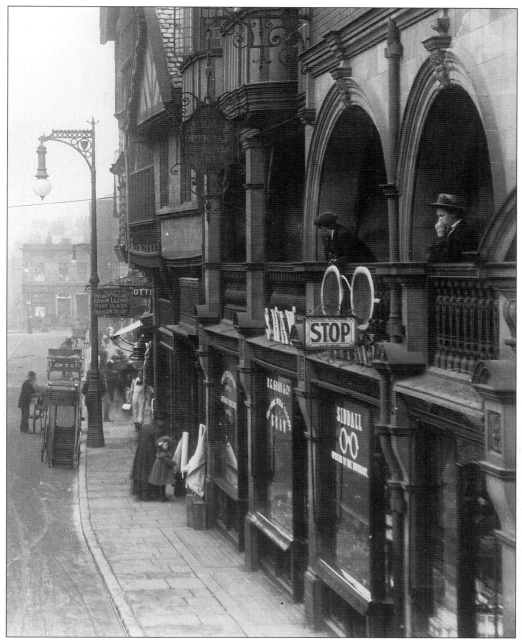

Here in this view of about 1910 we have Donald's the chemist, Siddall the optician, (established since 1815), Shaw's the ironmongers and the *Cheshire Observer* offices. The mother and the little girl are examining the display in H. Jefferson's (draper and hosier) window.

Before being demolished in June 1863, twenty of the twenty-six stagecoach services coming to the city each day operated from the Feathers Hotel on the right. In the centre of the street was the horse-drawn cab rank. There was also a wooden shelter for the cab men.

Bridge Street between 1880 and 1892. On the corner of Commonhall Street a large notice board advertises W.M. Williams, plumber and handyman of all descriptions and Barlow & Son, wine and spirit merchants at the Old Vaults. Underneath the Dutch Houses were Hooleys, tallow chandlers and Davies' sweet shop.

This is the old Saddle Inn at the corner of Bunce Street and Grosvenor Street, before it was developed into the present building. The landlord in 1860 was Reuben Smith and in 1874, A. Bernhardt.

Grosvenor Street in 1902. On the left are: Simson, saddler, E.F. Edge, plumber, J. Jarvis, florist, P. Dodd, Castle Dining Rooms, J.J. Sampney, Kings Head. On the right: Nelson and Sons, British and Colonial Meat Company, R. Newns, hairdresser, and the entrance to the White Bear Stables.

The Falcon, Lower Bridge Street in 1874 with Little Cuppin Street on the right. The shops to the left are: Mr H. Walsh's, boot and shoe manufacturers, S. Speeds, corn warehouse and the White Bear Inn.

At number 70 Lower Bridge Street W.S. Garrad had dining rooms in 1915-1916 which, in 1919-1920 were called the Mons Cafe, as shown on this advertisement card. The other shops were, at No. 68, H. Snelson, newsagent and tobacconist, at Nos 64-66, E.T. Jones, ironmonger and at No. 62, F.A. Betteridge, wood turner.

In Lower Bridge Street, Tudor House on the right is reputed to be the oldest building in Chester. When Tudor houses were built, it was during a time when superstition and fear of witchcraft were prevalent and a live cat was sometimes put into the walls of the house during construction to 'protect' the building from the spells of witches.

This close up view shows two shops occupying Tudor House. The narrow entry between it and the Feather's Inn was called Hawarden Castle Entry and led to Albion Street.

The Bear & Billet and Bridgegate are decorated, as was the rest of Chester, to celebrate the coronation of Edward VII which was due to take place on 26 June 1902. Because of the King's ill health however, the coronation did not take place until August of that year. Chester, like many other places, went ahead with the events planned nevertheless.

Taken from the Dee Bridge, this view looks back up Lower Bridge Street. The writer of this postcard says he has not yet enlisted and sends greetings to his old mates in Sheffield. His message refers to recruitment in the First World War.

The Fountain, once a feature of Bridge Street, was put here in 1859 when the mayor was Mr Meadows Frost who owned flour mills in Chester and Ellesmere Port.

On the left are Jackson's Gold Medal Tea Stores, established in 1849, and Edwin Lloyd, Central Supply Stores and daily suppliers of first class fruit. On the right is J. Brickland, fish and game supplier.

This photograph was taken shortly after this corner was rebuilt in 1888. The only shop that appears to be occupied is R. Catley, watchmaker. The empty premises to the right were later occupied by Huke's Library and bookshop, (see page 48).

This is Eastgate Street in 1874 and, in the centre of the street, is a horse cab rank similar to the one in Bridge Street, (see page 30).

This view looks back into Eastgate Street before the Jubilee Clock was installed. The first shop on the right is Huke's Library and bookshop, which can be seen in more detail on page 48.

When a horse tram arrived at the station terminus the driver went into the front entrance of the Albion Hotel and emerged with a length of chain about nine inches long which he laid in the groove of one of the tracks. The horse would then drag the vehicle off the track, turn it around over the stone setts and on to the other track – a horse tram turntable!

On fine mornings the carriages, with coachmen and footmen, could be seen standing outside Brown's or Beckett's while their owners or their wives went shopping for clothes, shoes, hats and the like at these exclusive shops.

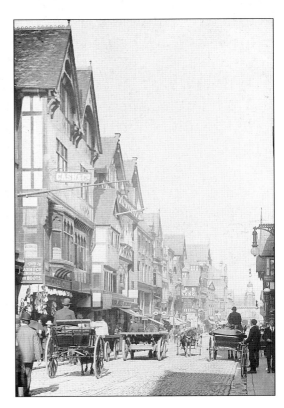

Later in the day, Eastgate Street, like all other streets in the city, would get jammed up with horse-drawn transport of every description.

Eastgate Street before the First World War. On the left is H.C. Houghton B.O.A, eyesight and spectacle specialist and late manager for Wood Abrahams of Liverpool. On the right is Bolland's Restaurant, 'the place to dine', accompanied by music supplied daily by The Trio.

Eastgate, festooned with flags and decorations for an unknown celebration in the late 1920s.

Next to the Liverpool Bank at the corner of St Werburgs Street can be seen the ornate structure of the Corn Exchange which was used as a cinema from 1909 until it closed down on Saturday 29 March 1924. Shows began at 7.00 pm and 9.00 pm; prices were 2d, 3d, 4d and 6d, seats could be reserved for 2d extra.

A room at the Kings Arms, advertised on the left, was set up as a council chamber where a drinking and a gambling club called The Honourable Incorporation used to meet in burlesque imitation of the city dignitaries. The furniture used by then is now in the Grosvenor Museum.

A picturesque view of a quiet day on Eastgate Row. The Dunne sisters were situated on the south side of the Row near its junction with the east side of Bridge Street Row.

Posing under the Jubilee Clock is still a
popular place for visitors having their
photographs taken.

This photograph of Eastgate was taken in the late 1930s.

This picture from the 1930s must revive memories for many. The horse-drawn coal delivery wagon, the stately Kardomah delivery van and Woolworths in the Corn Exchange were all familiar sights.

44

The time is five minutes to eight in the morning and most of the transport is horse drawn: the milk float, the farmer with his loaded cart and a pony and cart awaiting its owner.

Although the motor transport with its chauffeurs are parked in Foregate Street, it is more than likely that their passengers are in the Grosvenor Hotel. The year is 1904 and the group are outside J.E. Brassey's.

The cyclist has just come through the Newgate from the direction of Little St John Street, a group of four houses that stood on the left and connected with St John Street. On the right is a shoeing forge, a waggonette proprietor's yard and Poynton's pipe works where churchwarden and other clay pipes were made.

Outside the Marlborough Inn in St Johns Street stands the Shrewsbury coach that still supplied a service to Chester hotels in the late nineteenth century.

The extensive graveyard on the north side of St John's in 1911. In the background is the ruined Thornton chancel.

The Anchorite's cell was constructed in 1358. This is it in 1907, before the Corporation purchased it in 1910 and made considerable alterations.

Huke's Library and Bookshop were in Foregate for a number of years. They later had a shop at the corner of Eastgate Street and Bridge Street and published very attractive postcards. Standing in the doorway is Mr Pearson.

Around the corner in Frodsham Street is Mr A.E. Dutton, standing outside his first shop with his employees. The shop later became Irwin's then the first Tesco in Chester. The business moved to its present premises in 1923, with a fourth generation of the family involved in the business.

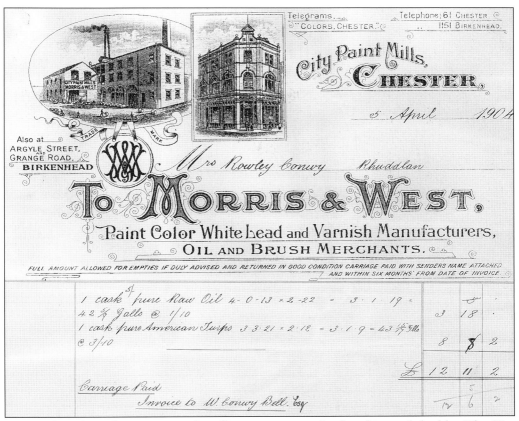

Newton has always been an area of small engineering works, foundries and the like. The City Paint Mills were at No. 25 Egerton Street.

The Ormonde Arms was situated at the end of Brook Street. In the background can be seen the archways of the General Railway Station. The licensee in 1900 was F.J. Jones and, from 1923 until 1939, it was W. Delmage.

The Nags Head in Foregate Street was originally the Chester Cocoa House and had its own promotional 'token coins' which could be spent on the premises.

On the north side looking towards City Road at No. 89 was W. Huke, chemist and dispensary; further along was William Price, wines and spirits.

Next door to the White Lion the signs would indicate a motor garage. For a few moments Foregate Street is quiet with not even a tram, enabling the children to pose in the middle of the road.

The original postcard of this view was published by a French firm in 1909. The view looks towards the Bars and shows a pawnbroker in a building which appears slope backwards!

The façade of the hotel before this, bore a legend that it was established in 1601 and the advertisement emphasizes this.

City Road was constructed by the various railway companies in 1864 with the City Council agreeing to adopt it after completion and also to pay for the building of a new canal bridge.

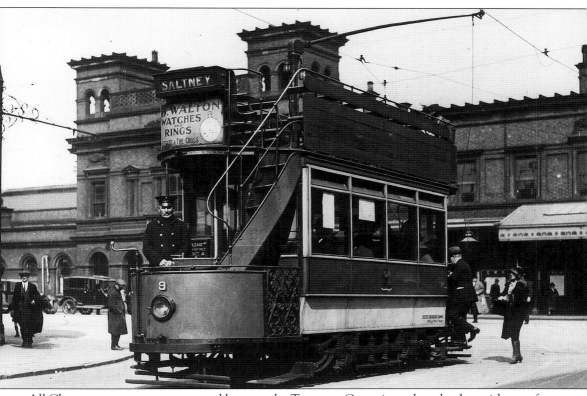

All Chester trams were open topped because the Tramway Committee thought that with a roof they would not pass under Eastgate. They were also one of the few tramways that would allow dogs on board. The dogs had to travel upstairs and pay the full passenger fare!

The *Daily Mail* poster mentions General Botha who was the Prime Minister of Transvaal and attended the Imperial Conference in England that year, so dating this scene. The bookstall and the use of buildings have been changed several times. Major alterations have taken place in recent years and now, only the steps are left.

On the extreme right can be seen the horse brakes of the Blossoms and the Grosvenor Hotels, awaiting patrons from incoming trains. The Blossoms' brake is in yellow and that of the Grosvenor in black; each had their drivers clad in splendid livery.

In 1906 a single decker was delivered to the corporation's tramways. It had reversed, fully enclosed platforms, but with only twenty seats and needing a crew of two. After trials it proved uneconomic. It was used on race days and was equipped with a snow plough and only used as required.

Two
Events, People
and Transport

In 1861, when scarcely a year old, the Queen Railway Hotel was largely destroyed by fire. The militia quickly arrived on the spot with the Chester fire engines. The Birkenhead and Crewe engines were also promptly telegraphed. Captain Humberston MP, the mayor and a body of volunteers assisted by the police, managed to save the plate and most of the furniture.

On 30 December 1862 the first Town Hall burned down. When the fire bell tolled, the news spread and a large crowd assembled. The engines had insufficient power to project the water and the spectators heaped abuse on members of the fire brigade.

An inspection of the Church Lads Brigade in 1905 in the Market Square, after which they proceeded to the Cathedral for a special service.

The state procession of the Lord Mayor and the Sheriffs of London on a visit to Chester on 16 April 1906. They are seen here walking to the Cathedral for a special service of thanksgiving.

After being met at Chester General Railway Station by the Duke of Westminster as Lord Lieutenant of Cheshire, the Prince and Princess of Wales paid their first visit to the city on 6 July 1908 as the Earl and Countess of Chester.

Arriving at the Town Hall in an open landau they received a tumultuous welcome from the citizens of Chester and the Prince inspected a guard of honour from the 3rd Welsh Brigade RFA, (Territorial) commanded by Major T.H. Wood.

This is the inauguration of Alderman D.L. Hewitt as Mayor of Chester in 1910. The following day, in the Town Hall, before attending a service in the Cathedral, he presented Branchman W. Staton with the medal of the National Fire Brigade Union for ten years service.

This is the procession of the new mayor, who had been inaugurated the previous day, Saturday, to a mayoral service in the Cathedral.

On one occasion the firemen accompanied the mayor into the Cathedral but in the middle of the service they were summoned to attend a fire. They were not invited inside again to take part in the ceremony. The mayor for 1907 was Alderman John Jones.

While building St Michael's Arcade in 1909 workmen discovered a Roman mosaic floor.

When the alarm bell was rung at night the horses had to be brought from Aldred's stables in Upper Northgate Street which caused some delay, but they made a brave show as they were led out of the station. The man on the back of the machine would be stoking up the furnace under the big steam boiler and the firemen, standing on each side, holding flaming torches and wearing their brass helmets. Superintendant Stone and one other man were the permanent staff; the remainder were volunteer part time members. This is the Prince of Wales Voluntary Fire Brigade outside their new headquarters in Northgate Street in 1901, second from the right is David Cross.

This is the head of a colourful parade of the Chester Co-operative Society Limited, marching past the Grosvenor Museum and the end of Bunce Street on the Co-operative's Fete and Gala Day, sometime between 1908 and 1912.

These ladies are celebrating the 21st Anniversary of the Chester Co-op Women's Guild. Second from the left in the back row is Edith Cross, who was their secretary for over forty years.

Reading out the proclamation of King George V on 9 May 1910 from the steps of the Town Hall in front of a large crowd of people.

Thousands of people flocked to Chester on King George V's Coronation Day. Here, opposite the Town Hall, a local band is playing popular tunes of the day.

Chester Infirmary Fete was held on the Roodee in October 1912. The maypole event was one of the afternoon's entertainments.

The Albert Wood wings extension of the infirmary was opened by King George V on 25 March 1914. At the same time he bestowed the title 'Royal' to its name.

On 29 May 1907 an advance party of the 3rd Battalion Cheshire (Militia), consisting of one officer and 300 men, left Chester by rail for Castleton, Derbyshire, to set up their annual camp. They were four weeks under canvas.

Chester Volunteers Starting for camp May '07

Handing over Their Old Colours at Chester Cathedral

The 1st Battalion Cheshire Regiment received new colours in July 1907. This shows the old ones being deposited in the Cathedral in October of the same year.

In 1914 an encampment was set up on Eaton Fields for the recruitment and training of personnel for the Royal Medical Corps. Seen here are Lance Corporal David Cross and a young boy bugler.

This is No. 4 Platoon, 'A' Company, 25th Cheshire Regiment before their departure for the battlefields of France. At the end of the Battle of Highwood on the Somme, there were only seven survivors.

This was the last reunion of the Metropolitan Sergeants' Technical Association, held in September 1914 at Chester Barracks.

The 5th Battalion Cheshire Regiment was mobilized on 5 August 1914, went first to Shrewsbury and then overseas to France in November. They fought gallantly at Ypres and the Somme. Their last action was between 27 September and 1 October 1918 at Canal du Nord.

A class from Hunter Street School for Girls in 1921. The head teacher was Miss M.A. Davies and the school had accommodation for 262 pupils.

A class from Victoria Road Infants School in 1924. Victoria Road today is divided by St Oswalds Way. The school still stands in the section of Victoria Road to Brook Street, but it is now a private school and called Abbey Gate School.

This was a large procession through the city's main streets in support of the Temperance Movement. The banners of the Dunham Hill contingent and the City Mission, Band of Hope, can clearly be seen.

The Band of Hope, on a horse-drawn float, are taking part in another Temperance Parade on 19 October 1921 in George Street, opposite the Temperance Hall.

George Street Methodist Sunday School Annual Field Day at Blacon, c. 1930. The elderly gentleman is Walter Vernon who rebuilt Chester Cross.

Teachers and members of George Street Sunday Bible Class in 1936.

The 'Hoop Gang' in 1931. The boys pose with their hoops, which were originally bicycle wheels. Each boy would name his hoop after his favourite motorcycle: Rudge, BSA or AJS. In the background is Allington Place.

The Sunday School Pageant was held every year, depicting themes from the history of the city. This is the May Queen Parade with the children dressed as Roman soldiers, marching down Bridge Street in 1931.

In 1931 the Duke and Duchess of York, (the future King George VI and Queen Elizabeth) came to Chester to visit the Royal Infirmary. They are seen here with the Mayor of Chester, the Bishop of Chester and officials and staff of the hospital.

This is a garden party at Upton Lawn, Upton, Chester, given by David Frost of the milling family. Evident in the picture are his father John Meadows Frost (Mayor of Chester 1913-1919) with his wife and two of David's aunts, Aggie and Mabel.

The London Midland and Scottish Railway employees at Chester General Railway Station had a brass band from 1919 until 1939. This photograph was taken in 1929 on the Town Hall steps.

This was the first mechanical delivery beer wagon to appear on the streets of the city. Displayed on the side of the wagon is the proud owner's name: J.T. Milne & Sons, ale and stout bottlers, Chester. The driver sitting on the left was George Cross.

The *Royal George* was one of the seven named buses in the Crosville fleet before the First World War. Some of the other names were, *Alma, Deva, Flying Fox* and *Busy Bee*. It was new in 1912, had an open rear platform and operated between Chester and New Ferry, travelling via Ellesmere Port.

During the First World War this Crosville bus, No. 19, was requisitioned by the Ministry of Defence to provide a service for the wounded soldiers between the General Railway Station and various hospitals in the city.

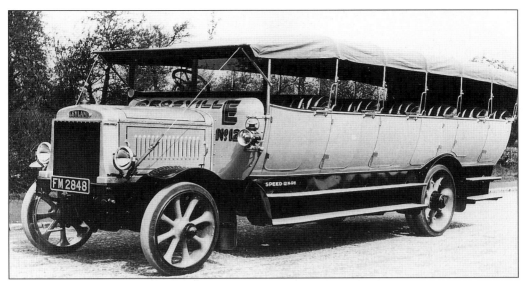

This Leyland was delivered to Crosville between 1924 and 1925. Being a charabanc, it was used for day excursions and group outings. Mr Joe Hudson, who had amalgamated his bus service with Crosville in 1922, became the manager for organising extended tours, which started in 1928.

There were transport services of various kinds operating from local villages and towns into Chester. This photograph shows the bus service between Chester and Ellesmere Port which was run by a local man, Mr J.M. Hudson, who was a councillor. It operated from 1919 until taken over by Crosville in 1922.

A view from the footbridge of the south end of Chester General Railway Station showing No. 46256 *Sir William Stanier FRS* on 6 June 1961. Note the array of ex-LNWR lower quadrant semaphore signals.

The ex-GWR County Class locomotive No. 1022, *County of Northampton*, at Chester General with a train from Birkenhead (Woodside) to London (Paddington) on 6 June 1961.

British Rail Standard Class 9F 2-10-0 No. 92126 passes under the magnificent ex-LNWR lower quadrant semaphore signal gantry which once adorned the north end of Chester General, on 17 June 1961.

The ex-GWR *County of Hampshire* sits quietly at the south end of Chester General while awaiting its train on 18 February 1961.

Northgate Station was opened in 1875 and was operated by the Cheshire Lines Committee. The billboard is advertising a day return to London for sixty shillings (£3). The station closed down at the end of the 1960s. (Lens of Sutton)

This is the DMU (Diesel Motorised Unit) about to leave Chester Northgate for Wrexham Central, via Sealand, on 18 February 1961.

Chester Football Club was built out of Chester Rovers and King's School Old Boys in 1884/5. At that time they rented a field in Faulkner Street, Hoole, then known as Bishop Field. After one or two other venues they moved, in 1904, to the ground in Whipcord Lane.

CHESTER FOOTBALL CLUB, LTD.

Secretary:
B. G. DICKIN,
73, Catherine St.,
CHESTER.

Tel. 706.

Curzon Rd Calmley *Apl 29th* 192*4*

Dear Sir,

Please note that you have been selected to play for Chester against *E Port Cement* on *Thursday May 1* at *Chester*. Train leaves ————— Station at ——. **Kick-off** *4 0* **p.m.** Notify me at once if you cannot play.

Yours truly,

B. G. DICKIN, Secretary.

This is the selection card that was sent to a Manchester man informing him that he had been selected to play for Chester against Ellesmere Port Cement Works Football Club, at Chester, on 1 May 1924. The kick off was at four o'clock.

Before a crowd of 15,000 on Chester Race Cup night in 1933, Chester FC beat Wrexham FC 2-0 to win the Welsh Cup. Present among the spectators were the Duke and Duchess of Westminster. Thus Chester FC regained the trophy after a lapse of twenty-five years.

A Chester FC team from the early 1950s. Back row, left to right: R. Moremont, P. Greenwood, T. Astbury, H. Treadgold, E. Lee, T. Tiltson, F. Hindle. Front row, left to right: W. Foulkes, J. Hankinson, G. Burgess and L. Devonshire.

This is Chester Nomads Amateur Football Club 1912/13. The club is still going strong today.

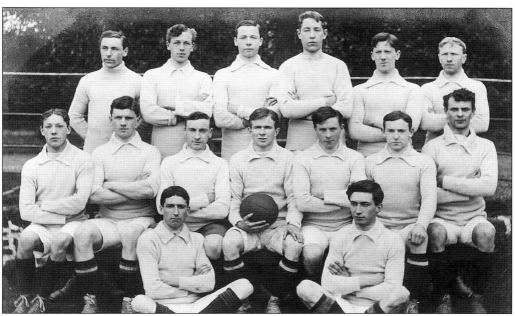

Rugby first started in Chester in 1870 but after some time died out. From time to time the city had teams and matches but not on a permanent basis. The rugger team pictured here, on 13 April 1910, represents the Seniors who beat their opponents, the Juniors, by thirty-one points to nil. Captain of the team was Hy Bell; sub captain was R. Stanley Wilson. Chester Rugby Club started in 1925. Its first match took place against Chester College at the YMCA ground in Sealand.

The 6th Battalion Cheshire Home Guards were formed on 22 May 1940. Its greatest trial was on the night of 28 November 1940 when high explosives and a land mine exploded over Handbridge, causing over 100 fires.

This is the funeral of Fireman Cyril Dutton on Tuesday 3 December 1940. He was killed during an air raid on the city while fire fighting in the area at the back of what is now Littlewoods. He died aged only twenty-five.

Number 610 (County of Chester) Squadron of the Auxiliary Air Force was formed in February 1936 at Hooton Park. It was originally a bomber unit and was equipped with Hawker Hart bombers, seen here at Hooton Park in 1937.

The same squadron was remustered as a fighter squadron in January 1938. Those gathered round the aircraft at Hooton Park, early in 1939, include: Leading Aircraftsman Evans, Flying Officer Smith, Pilot Officer A.J. Mason, Leading Aircraftsman Jones. In October the squadron moved to RAF Wittering, Northamptonshire.

During the Battle of Britain No. 610 (County of Chester) Squadron operated from Biggin Hill. Here we see Squadron Leader John Ellis looking at the remains of a German 109 Messerschmitt shot down near Biggin Hill in 1940. Also present at the scene are Flying Officer Lamb and Pilot Officer Rees, on the left.

Guardsman Eric Cross was awarded the Military Medal by King George VI on the morning of VE Day. Outside Buckingham Palace that night he stood alongside an ATS officer who was with two Guards officers; he recognised the ATS officer as none other than the future Queen of England.

The Cross family reunion. After five years of war the Cross family – Wilfred, Vivian, Rhona and Eric – pose for a family portrait.

On his visit to Chester in February 1971, Prince Charles unveiled a plaque at the new fire station. Afterwards he was shown around the building and introduced to the fire officers by Chief Fire Officer Harry Sheldon who is seen second from the left.

Three
The River Dee

Coming from the south bank just beyond the bridge and travelling in a diagonal line to the north bank, five feet below the surface of the river, is Watling Street and the Roman ford across the Dee.

Eccleston ferry is recorded in the Domesday Book. The Sergeants of the Dee were the Grosvenor family and, as such, provided the ferry boat and received the tolls. The first vehicle ferry was operated by ropes. The ferry house seen here was swept away by floods in 1887.

The new ferry house was built higher up the bank to protect it from floods. A larger ferry boat was built at the same time because of the increase in transport and was operated by chains.

Seen here in the early 1900s, the ferry boat is preparing to offload on the opposite bank. The lady and the small boy in the sailor suit are also in the picture below.

Here is 'Jimmy the boats', the ferryman standing by the chain system that works the boats. In the background a pleasure boat is heading back to the Groves landing stage.

The Chester Regatta is the oldest in the country. Regattas have been held here since before 1814 and this print depicts the one of 1854. The Royal Chester Rowing Club received royal patronage from Queen Victoria in 1840, which was reaffirmed by Queen Elizabeth II in 1974.

These are members of the Royal Chester Rowing Club who won the North of England Head of the River Race in 1952. Stroke: W.L.S. Wallace; No. 4, W.B. Hiscocks; No. 7, D.A. Cross; No. 3, G.N. Pointer; No. 6, R.E. Buckley; No. 2, K.G.P. Clemence; No. 5, J.W. Pearson; Bow, J.G. Wincent; Cox, M. Leese.

The Royal Chester Rowing Club Crew display the Head of the River Pennant which they won jointly with Durham University in 1954, the same year in which they won the Clinker Pennant.

The Clemence family, members of the Royal Chester Rowing Club spanning three generations, are pictured here in 1964: bow, G.H.P. aged 17, G.T.A. aged 49, K.G.P.C. aged 41 (No. 3) and T.H.Y.C. aged 83 (stroke).

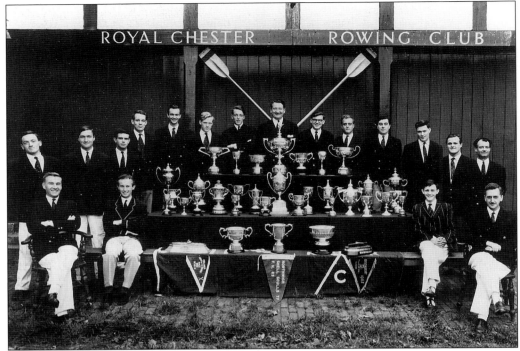

In 1963 members of the Royal Chester Rowing Club won numerous rowing events throughout the country and this is a display of the trophies collected.

It is July 1904 and the boats are moored on the shoreline of Sandy Lane. On the back of this picture the sender asks the recipient if they recognise anyone in the boat.

This was the first suspension bridge linking Queen's Park with the Groves. Built in 1851 by James Dredge of Bath for Mr E. Gerrard who owned the land in Handbridge, it was replaced by the present bridge on 18 April 1923.

It is Regatta week 1905 and the crowds on the banks watch what appears to be a lifeboat and may not have noticed the high diver from the suspension bridge.

Occupying pride of place on the river were the two red funnel steamers *Bend-Or* and *Ormonde*, named after two of the first Duke of Westminster's race horses. These craft took turns in carrying a three piece orchestra; three brothers known as the Massa Brothers, one of whom played the harp. The river trip on a summer's day, with their music in the background, supplemented by strawberries and cream at the tea house at Eccleston Ferry, was a most enjoyable outing. The proprieters were the Dee Steamboat Company, managed by Mr Bradbury. The top boat is the *Ormonde* and the bottom one, the *Bend-Or*.

PICTORIAL POST CARD.

THE ADDRESS TO BE WRITTEN ON THIS SIDE

THIS SPACE, AS WELL AS THE BACK, MAY BE USED FOR COMMUNICATIONS. (See Postal Regulations.)

THE ADDRESS ONLY TO BE WRITTEN HERE.

AFFIX HALFPENNY STAMP.

Sailings for May, June, July, and August.

The Dee Steamboat Co.'s
"BEND OR" and "ORMONDE."

THE above Company is the only one authorised by His Grace the Duke of Westminster, to run their Steamers regularly to Eccleston and to Eaton.

TIMES OF SAILING (Sundays excepted)

	a.m.	a.m.	a.m.	p.m.	p.m.	p.m.	p.m.	p.m.	p.m.	p.m.
CHESTER ... dep.	9.0	10.30	11.30	1.0	1.30	2.45	3.30	4.30	5.30	7·0
Eccleston Ferry .	9.50	11.20	12.30	1.50	2.20	3.35	4.20	5.20	6.20	7·50
IRON BRIDGE arr.	10.15	11.45						5.45		
IRON BRIDGE dep.	10.15	11.45						5.45		
Eccleston Ferry ...	10.40	12.10	12.35	1.50	2.20	3.35	4.30	6.10	6.45	7·50
CHESTER .. arr.	11.30	1.0	1.25	2.40	3.10	4.25	5.20	7.0	7.35	8·30

Weather and other causes permitting.

FARES—Chester to Eccleston. **6d.** Single; **9d.** Return.
,, Iron Bridge. **8d.** ,, **1s.** ,,
SPECIAL TERMS MADE FOR PARTIES.

*The Last Trip will run during the Months of June & July only.

All Letters to be addressed to

An advertisement postcard for the Dee Steamboat Company's two boats, *Bend-Or* and *Ormonde* in the early 1900s. The postcard also provides information about fares and sailing times.

The SS *Volunteer* and another boat, *The Lady Beatrice*, both had buff funnels and belonged to Mr Williams, who owned a rival company. There was also a trio of boats with white funnels which were owned by the Chester Boat Company (Capner's).

The Dee froze over in 1895, on the 8 February 1917, and on 17 February 1929. Mark Cook, who had his studio on City Walls, was present to record the latter for the benefit of future generations.

It is 1895 and there has been a heavy frost, the first step to the river freezing over. Here are some young people putting on their ice skates. The old Deva Inn visible in the background.

Once again, photographer Mark Cook was on hand to capture on film the antics on the frozen river in 1929. Everyone is warmly wrapped up against the cold.

Although not wearing skates, members of the Cheshire Constabulary are on standby to lend a hand if needed on the frozen river in 1895.

An old advertisement informs that, 'Steamers ply between Chester and Eccleston (3 and a half miles); fares: 6d single, 9d return. Also between Chester and the Iron Bridge (5 and a half) miles; fares: 8d single, 1s return. On Bank Holidays all tickets are single.'

No room to spare and what a variety of men's headgear!

The causeway, a weir across the River Dee, was built by Hugh Lupus the first Earl of Chester who, in 1093, granted the right to build the Abbey Mill at the Dee Bridge.

MILL WEIR & BRIDGE GATE. CHESTER.

The weir was so shaped that the impounded water would flow under the last two arches of the bridge and supply water power to the waterwheels of the mill. This postcard is postmarked 27 February 1903.

The outlet of water shown here, flowing into the King's Pool below the salmon cage, at one time operated two different mills. One of these later became the Snuff Mill, owned by Messrs T. Nicholls and the other, Topham's Mill, which stood on the east side. The lane to the bridge was called Tophams Lane.

Nicholl's Tobacco Company was established in 1780. Their head office and factory were situated on the Handbridge side of the weir. This is an advertisement card for the firm.

This group of ladies is engaged in shredding tobacco leaves as part of the process of making snuff at Nicholl's snuff mills, sometime during 1930/31.

Judging from the number of delivery vans, it would appear that Nicholl's Tobacco Company had a thriving business in the 1930s.

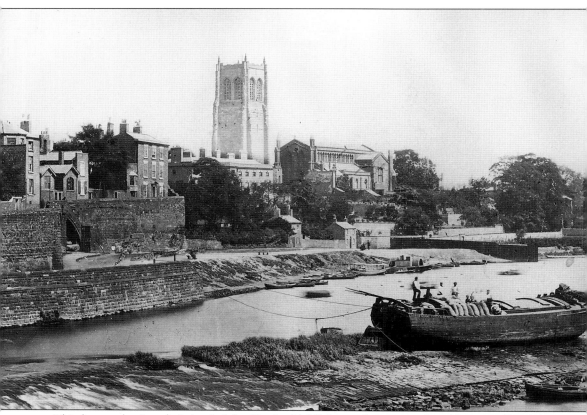

This barge, the *Joseph*, is loaded for Guiders' Mill, better known as the old Dee mills. If there was a cargo for this mill, the lock gate from the Shropshire Union Canal into the Dee could only be opened on a flood tide. To navigate the flat, two extra men had to be sent with long poles to keep the flat end on the tide and keep her straight. Rings were set in the wall of the mill quay; the hand with the flat had to stand 'forrard' with a rope attached, to slip into the ring. The scene above shows what happened as a result of missing it – being carried away under the bridge and stranded on top of the causeway as the tide receded. It required nearly all the cart horses in Chester to pull her off.

At one time a familiar figure at the mill was an old, miller whose beard, wide-brimmed hat and long smock were well plastered with flour dust. He would invariably be found standing on the loading platform adjoining the bridge, ready to have a word with passers by.

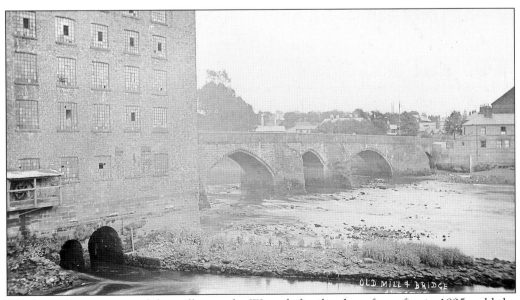

The last private owners of the mill were the Wrench family who, after a fire in 1895, sold the ruins and the river rights to the Corporation. Another fire in 1910 resulted in the remaining buildings being demolished.

The law forbids net fishing on the River Dee on Fridays, Saturdays and Sundays. From a boundary in the estuary to Chester, a draft net is used. To operate it, one fisherman takes an end of the line on the bank upstream while his partner rows his boat, with the net folded over the stern, across the river. When about three-quarters of the way over, the net is paid out and the boat turns downstream until opposite the landing place. Meanwhile the fisherman on the bank draws inwards, the boatman doing the same until the net itself appears. Then the bank man hauls his rope down towards the landing place and, if they are lucky, there will be some salmon trapped in the mesh of the net.

The fishermen had their own particular spots to fish from, all with their own names such as, Littlewood, Under the Hills, Lane End, Crane and Marshead. There were once fourteen fishing places within a distance of two miles of the old Dee Bridge, now there are only six.

Seen here are Edward and Ned Buckley with their brother Ted, who were all fishermen of Handbridge. In 1947 they made a record catch with their draft net of forty-seven salmon.

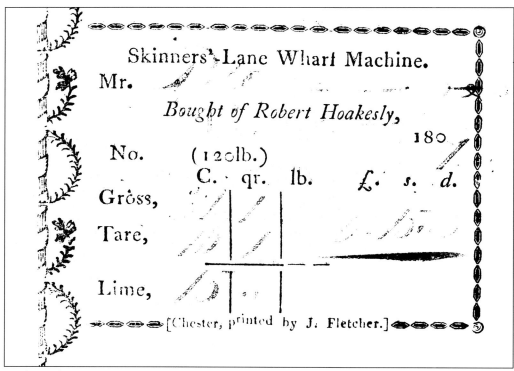

Skinners' Lane Wharf Machine.

Mr.

Bought of Robert Hoakesly,

180

No.   (120lb.)

C.   qr.   lb.   £.   s.   d.

Gross,

Tare,

Lime,

[Chester, printed by J. Fletcher.]

In the early nineteenth century a road called Skinner's Lane ran between the castle wall and the river. It housed the workshops of animal skinners and an acid factory. In the early 1830s the county authorities acquired this industrial area, demolished it and extended the city walls to enclose it. The wall now makes a right angled turn to the south east and drops to the level of Castle Drive. This toll ticket for Skinners Lane Wharf, is dated 1809.

The Grosvenor Toll Bridge was operated by the Dee Bridge Commissioners and remained as such until 1885. The toll per person was 1d, with additional charges for vehicles and animals. There was a special rate for tramway traffic. The toll booths were situated on the Overleigh side.

This is the second railway bridge over the River Dee at the Roodee, taken on 26 June 1901. A fatal accident occurred here on 24 May 1847. When the 6.15 pm train from Chester to Wrexham was crossing over the Dee on the first bridge, the third arch broke and the train fell into the river, killing five people.

This sketch appeared in the *Illustrated London News* on 9 May 1846. Apart from the races theme, it is unique because it shows the Row that was on the west side called the Shoemakers Row, which was demolished in the 1890s.

When King Edward VII arrived at Chester General Railway Station, he was met by the Mayor of Chester, Alderman J. Jones and other officials, including the General Officer Western Command, Sir Charles Burnett KCB. With an escort of the Eaton Squadron of the Cheshire Yeomanry they proceeded through the city first to Eaton Hall, then later to the Roodee.

This is the Chester Cup for 1908, which was won by *Glacis*, owned by Lord Derby and ridden by F. Wooton. The writer of the postcard from which this is copied says that she was 'near to the king'.

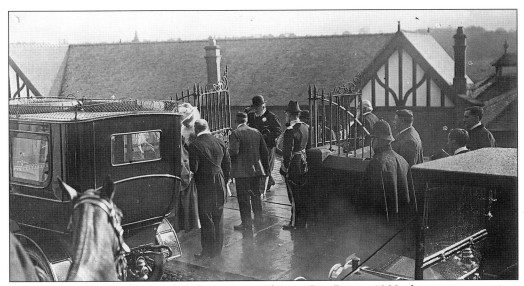

When King Edward VII attended the races on Chester Cup Day in 1908, the race was run in a heavy downpour. A special royal box was erected in the County Stand, handsomely furnished by Messrs Brown and Company.

Here a group of 'gentry' cross over the racecourse in 1906 to the paddock, which in those days was situated in the centre of the course.

The Duke of Westminster's horse *Troutbeck* is led to the scales. As far back as 1780, the Eaton Stud was established by John Richard, first Earl Grosvenor for the purpose of breeding high class racers. As an owner, the Duke of Westminster won 344 races with a total prize value of £301,614.

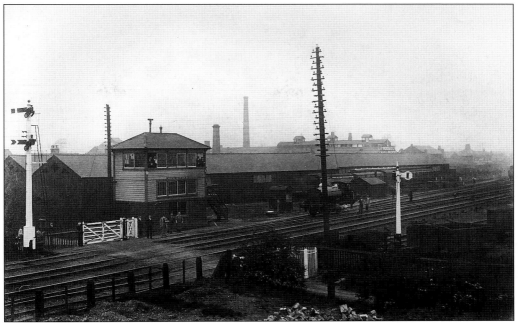

Further down the Dee, Saltney Quay was controlled by this signal box at Saltney Dee Junction. This view in the early 1900s also shows in the background the Great Western Railway's carriage and wagon works. The little shunting engine probably replaced the shunting horse seen in the photograph below.

This bridge is at Saltney and carries the coastal railway that goes between Chester and Holyhead. The main scene shows the Great Western Railway lines heading off to the right to Saltney Quay on 26 June 1901.

Saltney Quay was the termination point of the Great Western branch line that came from Wrexham along the Alyn Valley. This railway carried coal, slate and other minerals for shipment to other parts of the country.

The Manifolds of Higher Ferry have been Dee fishermen for over 200 years. In the 1840s William Manifold became the river supervisor for the River Dee Company. The family operated the free ferry for many years. Their boat, *Margaret*, was built by Arthur Howard at Taylor's Yard, Chester, in 1923.

112

Four
The Environs
of the City

Near to the main entrance of Overleigh Cemetery this tram has been stopped especially for the photographer. The cemetery was designed by T.M. Penson in the late 1840s. Buried here is Mary Jones, the mother of thirty-three children, including fifteen sets of twins, in the 1800s. In another grave nearby lies Edward Langtry, husband of Lily Langtry, a one time mistress of King Edward VII.

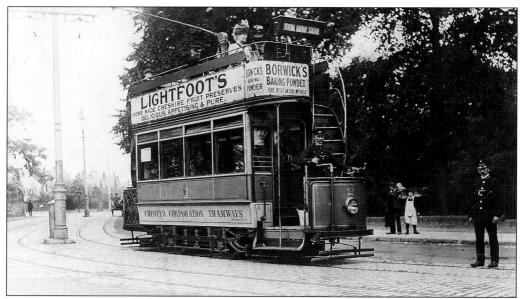

This is a No. 2 tram in Overleigh Road heading for the Grosvenor Bridge. When trams were passing over the bridge, the frequent high winds forced the conductors to keep hold of the trolley ropes so that the tram did not stop.

At the end of a two mile long avenue with trees on either side, are the Golden Gates, which date back to the beginning of the eighteenth century. In 1880 the clock tower was installed with a Belgian carillon of bells which played forty-eight different tunes.

During the Second World War, Eaton Hall was used as a hospital for officers looked after by the Red Cross and later. When Dartmouth Naval College was fire bombed it was transferred to the hall to become a naval college called HMS *Britannia*.

Earl Grosvenor was the four year old only son and heir of the second Duke. He died from appendicitis after a week's illness because the operation was performed too late. The family funeral took place on 16 February 1909 in the church at Eccleston. His godfather, King Edward VII, sent a message of sympathy to his friend Bendor.

Seen here during his stay at Eaton Hall in the Autumn of 1907, is the King of Spain with the Duke of Westminster and members of the Cheshire hounds.

Outside the magnificent stable block, guests and staff are awaiting the arrival of someone, but whom?

In 1896 the first Duke decided to have a narrow gauge railway built to connect Eaton Hall with Balderton Station at Kinnerton, three miles away.

As on all big estates, an important asset was the estate's own fire service. This is the Eaton Hall Fire Brigade ready for action. An impressive sight!

Here are members of the Duke of Wellington, Handbridge, Fishing Club between 1900 and 1905. The pub formerly stood at the corner of Queens Park Road and Handbridge Hill.

Handbridge Brickfields FC. This is the team that won the Runcorn Cup (Junior) in 1923/24. They won by six goals to nil. Back row, from the left: W. Lloyd, F. Price, J. Gerrard. Middle row: D. Chime, A. Hoult, J. Holyoak, ? Wainwright. Front row: ? Jenkins, ? Dain, T. Jones, ? Hamner, G. Gunson, ? Chester.

In the old graveyard at Eccleston village are buried members of the Grosvenor family, alongside the ruins of a former parish church. Five Dukes of Westminster are buried in ordinary graves with simple headstones.

When Sir Brian Horrocks was GOC Western Command, he was visited by his former commander and friend, Field Marshall B. Montgomery. Local children from Eccleston and Handbridge were quickly on the scene to pay tribute to the famous Second World War hero.

This was the old Brewer's Arms, Liverpool Road, Upton, which first appeared in the 1917 Trade Directory. When the present building was constructed it retained the same name until 1954. Nicknamed the 'Frog' after the stone frogs at the entrance, it eventually changed its name to The Frog and is now called The Frog and Firkin.

In 1905 the village of Upton held their garden fete in the grounds of Bache Hall, on the Liverpool Road.

A group of children pose for a local photographer in a street in Hoole at the turn of the century.

Sumpter Pathway, Hoole in about 1900.

The provision shop of Fred Ellis in Cecil Street, Hoole. This photograph was taken in November 1910 and shows Fred and his wife with their eldest daughter. He says on the back of the postcard that his wife gave birth to another daughter on the 'thirteenth of this month' and that he is going to call her Esther after his mother.

Hoole FC, 1928/29. Back row: Jim O'Reilly, Bill Morgan, T. Davenport. Middle row: Taff Doran, Bob Meacock, Ralph Short. Front row: G. Duckers, Bob Woods, Bob Broughton, E. Broughton, E. Brown, Tom Smith.

This was part of the first section of the Chester canal to be completed in January 1775. The barge is beneath the Northgate Bridge, heading down to the Northgate Locks, (below). The locks were constructed in 1795 as a staircase of three locks, to replace one of five that originally went into a tidal basin that connected with the River Dee.

VIEW OF RAILWAY, ROAD, AND CANAL FROM THE WALLS, CHESTER.

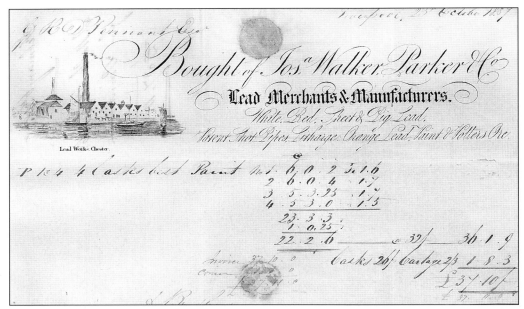

The leadworks were established in 1799 and the Shot Tower is still a prominent feature today. Much of the lead was supplied by the Halkyn Lead Mines at Flint, which were owned by the Grosvenor family from the seventeenth century until 15 December 1911. Lead shot is still made today for sports cartridges.

Looking towards the old Cow Lane Bridge, jutting out on the right, is Griffith's Mill, which was demolished in 1979. Griffith's had a provender stores in Lower Bridge Street.

Heading into the city and just outside Boughton Post Office, the tram has stopped to pick up passengers. The Boughton branch tram lines, on the left, went up Tarvin Road as far as the Bridge Inn, (see page 126).

Here is an inward Chistleton tram at Boughton Cross in 1904. One can't help feeling sorry for the tram driver, exposed to the wintry elements. Notice the side board advertising the Northgate Brewery.

The Market Square omnibus passes the Bridge Inn on the Tarvin Road as it returns to the city. In 1910 the landlord of the Bridge Inn was J.T. Milne. The side board shows Liverpool Road so the route must have been a circular one.

About the Authors

Michael Day was born in Chester and educated locally and started collecting photographs of Chester and Ellesmere Port in 1979. Most of the photographs in this book are part of his personal collection of images. A commercial photographer by trade, Michael now lives in Childer Thornton, Wirral with his wife and their son Francis. Together they run a photographic library of vintage images from all parts of the UK and worldwide, supplying photographic prints for both framing and publication.

Most of the photographs in this book are available as hand finished sepia photographs. For further details contact Michael and Ruth Day. Tel: 0151 339 5422.

Pat O'Brien was born in 1924, the youngest son of a distinguished soldier, Captain D. O' Brien, DCM, MSM. Educated in Dublin, he joined HM Forces in 1942 and saw active service in Sicily, Italy and Holland with the Parachute Regiment, eventually being taken POW at Arnhem. He has been researching local history since 1963. After early retirement from Burmah Oil Refinery in 1981, he became a Blue Badge Guide of Chester, an Accredited Guide of Chester Cathedral and a registered tutor of local history at West Cheshire College.

Pat has compiled three books in the *Archive Photographs* series: *Ellesmere Port* (1994), *Around Bebington* (1995) and *Burton to Heswall* (1996).

Acknowledgements

We would like to acknowledge and thank all those people who have helped to make this book possible by lending photographs and supplying valuable information:

Mr Bob Craven, Mr Eric Cross, A.H. Dutton and Son, Mrs K. Goulborn, Mr B. Hickey, Mr Ron Hignett, Miss A. Hodgson, Mrs G. Jackson, Lens of Sutton, Mr Mike Lister (railway historian and author), Mr Arthur Moorcroft, Mr Len Morgan (local historian), the late Mr Harry Major, Mr Ray Mulligan (local history tutor), F.N. Smith, Mr Lionel Smith, Mr John Whittingham (author and railway historian), the editor of the *Chester Chronicle*, Jim Brakell and the staff of Chester Reference Library and the City and County Record Offices.

A very special thank you to: Keith Osborne, Vice President of the Royal Chester Rowing Club and the committee for permission to copy photographs from their archives and for supplying information about them, and to George Frost, Steward of the Club, for all his help. If we have omitted anyone please accept our thanks and our apologies.